Stalwarts of Steam

Stalwarts of Steam

Roy Avis

Silver Link Publishing Ltd

First published in 2005

British Library Cataloguing in Publication Data

A catalogue record for this book is available from the British Library.

ISBN 1 85794 260 4

Silver Link Publishing Ltd
The Trundle
Ringstead Road
Great Addington
Kettering
Northants NN14 4BW

Tel/Fax: 01536 330588
email: sales@nostalgiacollection.com
Website: www.nostalgiacollection.com

Printed and bound in Great Britain

Front cover **Barrow Hill:** Running through rural scenery in an area of Derbyshire that has been scarred by coal-mining and other industries, No 6233 *Duchess of Sutherland* gets under way again after a water stop with a Derby to York train. *3 April 2003*

Back cover **Twerton:** The railway through Bath Spa was built to ensure the greatest degree of harmony with the local architecture. Hidden for many years behind lineside trees, the ornate tunnel portal can now be seen again from this angle, following recent clearance of the embankment. Locomotive No 73096 bursts into view, at the head of a London Victoria to Bristol Temple Meads train. *8 May 2003*

Page 1 **Cockwood Harbour:** No 3440 *City of Truro* passes with a Bristol Temple Meads to Paignton special, the first of two excursions to commemorate the locomotive's unauthenticated 102mph steam record, descending Wellington bank with the Ocean Mail train of 9 May 1904. It was not possible to run the following day, the actual centenary, due to engineering works, and the return working for the engine was made two days later. *8 May 2004*

Page 2 **Moorswater:** Nos 6024 *King Edward I* and 5029 *Nunney Castle* head west with an Exeter St David's to Par train. Completely rebuilt, the masonry arches of the new viaduct stand next to the moss-clad ruins of the Cornwall Railway's original timber structure. *23 April 2005*

Title page **Fenny Compton:** The only remaining section of the former Stratford-upon-Avon & Midland Junction Railway runs from here to the Ministry of Defence establishment at Kineton, a distance of just over 3 miles. Viewed from the old S&MJR platform, No 60009 passes with a Paddington to Derby train. *9 March 1995*

Left **Kettering Junction:** A photograph taken using an old pre-war Kodak camera, soon after the LMS had become the London Midland Region of British Railways. Locomotive No 48371 passes with a mixed goods on the down slow line. The semaphore signals survived until December 1987, but No 48371 was withdrawn at 8A Edge Hill shed on 14 October 1967, and stored there until April 1968; it was scrapped by Buttigiegs of Newport (South Wales) in June of that year. *Circa 1949*

Contents

Preface

Since operational steam on British Railways ceased, most of the water supply facilities and access points for the loading of coal have been dispensed with, and there are now only a handful of footplatemen possessing the firing skills, driving experience and stamina required to keep locomotives running with heavily loaded trains over the national railway network.

In addition, for main line steam to continue it has to comply with the Railway Safety & Standards Board requirements: all locomotives must now have TPWS (Train Protection and Warning System) and a date has been set for the mandatory fitting of OTMR (On Train Monitoring and Recording) – the so-called 'black box' technology. It had been hoped that there would be an exemption from this for steam.

Nevertheless, through the enthusiastic enterprise of locomotive owners and tour promoters, together with the whole-hearted co-operation of the train operating companies involved, steam can still be seen on Network Rail in the 21st century.

Great Western Railway
locomotives

'City' Class

Left **Scarborough:** Back on the national railway network following fund-raising by *Steam Railway* magazine to pay for heavy maintenance and the renewal of its boiler certificate to MT276 standard, locomotive No 3440 departs for York with the return working of a special day excursion train.

MT276 is the specification for overhaul and re-tubing of steam locomotives to main line levels of operation, with a boiler certificate for seven years. An extension of three years can be obtained provided that a further re-tube and examination is carried out before the certificate expires. *7 June 2004*

Below **York:** Withdrawn for preservation in March 1931, *City of Truro* returned to the main line in 1957 to haul a series of special trains, and was brought out of retirement again in 1985, for the Great Western '150' celebrations. Now back on Network Rail for a further sortie, No 3440 arrives with the empty coaching stock of a Scarborough day-tripper. *12 June 2004*

Dawlish: Back in May 1904, when 'Truro' made its epic record-breaking run with the Ocean Mail, a new land speed record of 97mph had been set only four days earlier, by Pierre de Caters, in a Mercedes 90 at Ostend, so it is just possible that the engine crew were the fastest men on earth at that time.

On a day when it later established more records, this time over the Devon banks, No 3440 skirts the coast at Horse Cove with a Bristol Temple Meads to Plymouth train. *27 November 2004*

Weaverthorpe: Closed as long ago as 1930, the station here carried various names: opened as Sherburn in 1845, it was re-named Wykeham in 1874, and finally Weaverthorpe in 1882. *City of Truro* passes with a York to Scarborough train. *7 June 2004*

'Hall' Class

Ascott-under-Wychwood: Blackening the Oxfordshire skies, No 4965 *Rood Ashton Hall* gets under way again, after a brief stop for operational purposes, with a Didcot to Birmingham Snow Hill special. *18 April 1999*

Washwood Heath: Main line signalling is controlled from the nearby Saltley power box, but more than 80 years after the demise of the former Midland Railway one of its cabins remains in use at the sidings, as No 4965 passes with a Christmas luncheon special. *17 December 2003*

Washwood Heath: Seen in abundance around Birmingham, gasometers will probably become part of our heritage, too, like No 4965 seen here passing the GEC Alsthom Metro-Cammell works with a festive tour. A bitterly cold wind blows the smoke away to the south, on a dull dank day. *17 December 2004*

Didcot: No 4965 *Rood Ashton Hall* and No 4936 *Kinlet Hall* double-head a special for Bristol Temple Meads along the former Great Western Railway main line. A well-known Oxfordshire landmark, the power station can be seen from many miles away across the Thames valley. *10 March 2001*

Droitwich Spa: *Kinlet Hall* heads a Birmingham Snow Hill to Didcot special. More than 50 years after nationalisation, former Great Western Railway infrastructure survives. *17 June 2000*

Henley-in-Arden: On the North Warwickshire line, formerly part of a through route to Cheltenham via Honeybourne, No 4965 passes with a Stratford-upon-Avon to Birmingham Snow Hill train. *18 July 1999*

'Castle' Class

Bristol Temple Meads: Built at Swindon in 1936, and introduced as *Drysllwyn Castle*, the following year No 5051 was re-named *Earl Bathurst* as a tribute to the former Great Western Railway director. It is leaving Bristol for Paignton with the 'Torbay Express', a special day excursion train to the seaside. *24 August 2003*

Twerton: No 5029 *Nunney Castle* emerges into the daylight with a London Victoria to Bristol Temple Meads train. Twerton Tunnel is only 264 yards in length, but is usually referred to as 'Twerton long tunnel' to avoid confusion with the nearby short Twerton Wood Tunnel. *20 March 2004*

Bristol Temple Meads: 'Mega-power' for the Devon banks, the now established pairing of Nos 5029 and 5051 leaves for Plymouth, double-heading a heavy 13-coach special day excursion train. *21 August 2004*

Moreton-in-Marsh: On the Cotswold line, *Nunney Castle* arrives with a Paddington to Worcester Shrub Hill train.
Lower-quadrant Great Western Railway semaphores prevail, but there are now UPVC windows in the signal box. *29 November 2003*

Fenny Compton: Just over 8 miles from Banbury, where water was taken, No 5029 heads north with a Didcot to Sheffield train. Sadly missed, the semaphores have now been superseded by fully automatic colour-light signals. *29 February 1992*

Culham: No 5029 *Nunney Castle* is seen again, this time with a Paddington to Worcester Shrub Hill special. It doesn't look very far, but the power station at Didcot is more than 2 miles away across the Thames valley. *14 July 2001*

Beeston Castle & Tarporley: The ubiquitous No 5029 is heading a Crewe, Chester and Holyhead train. There is a flourishing cattle market here, and the Shropshire Union Canal provides a popular tourist attraction, but Network Rail has abandoned plans to re-open the station. *28 October 2000*

'King' Class

Liskeard: The signals were 'on' as the train approached, but Nos 6024 *King Edward I* and 5029 *Nunney Castle* just avoided coming to a stand with a Par to Exeter St David's special when the line ahead cleared at the last moment. Hidden from view at the bottom of the hillside, the steeply graded loop line to the Moorswater and Looe branch passes through the valley beneath the viaduct. *23 April 2005*

Above **Crowdundle:** Built to allow the farmer to get his cows from one side of the line to the other, the magnificent occupation bridge spans a very deep cutting. Locomotive No 6024 is heading south with a Carlisle to Crewe train. *14 March 1998*

Right **Worcester Tunnel Junction:** *King Edward I* erupts into action with a train for Birmingham Snow Hill. Fortunately it's a Sunday afternoon, and not wash-day, so there are no clothes hanging out to dry! Looking out across the city, the tall slim spire of St Andrew's is in silhouette against the distant Malvern Hills. *31 March 2002*

'4300' Class

Stourbridge Junction: Built at Swindon in 1932, to a modified Churchward design embodying a side-window cab and other detail changes, 2-6-0 No 7325 arrives at first light for an early morning departure with a Bristol Temple Meads train. *4 November 1995*

Harrow-on-the-Hill: Simultaneous departures are made by No 7325, with a special for Watford, and Pannier Tank No 9466, with an Amersham train.

London Underground is not a 'light railway', and other train operating companies have access to some sections, including Chiltern Railways, which provides an intensive Marylebone to Aylesbury service over Metropolitan and Network Rail lines. Running powers on the Metropolitan were originally obtained more than 100 years ago by the Great Central Railway, when its London Extension, from Annesley Junction to Quainton Road, was built. *27 May 1996*

Chorleywood: It's a warm day and there is not much visible sign of effort from the locomotive on the long northbound climb through the Chilterns, but the harsh bark of the exhaust could be heard well before the train came into view. No 7325 is heading a Watford to Amersham special. *25 May 1996*

Chorleywood: This is a splendid stretch of line, and there was some fast running down the grade by No 7325 with an Amersham to Watford train. The preserved Metropolitan electric locomotive No 12 *Sarah Siddons* is included in the formation to provide braking for the air-braked coaching stock, as the steam engine is vacuum-braked only. *19 May 1996*

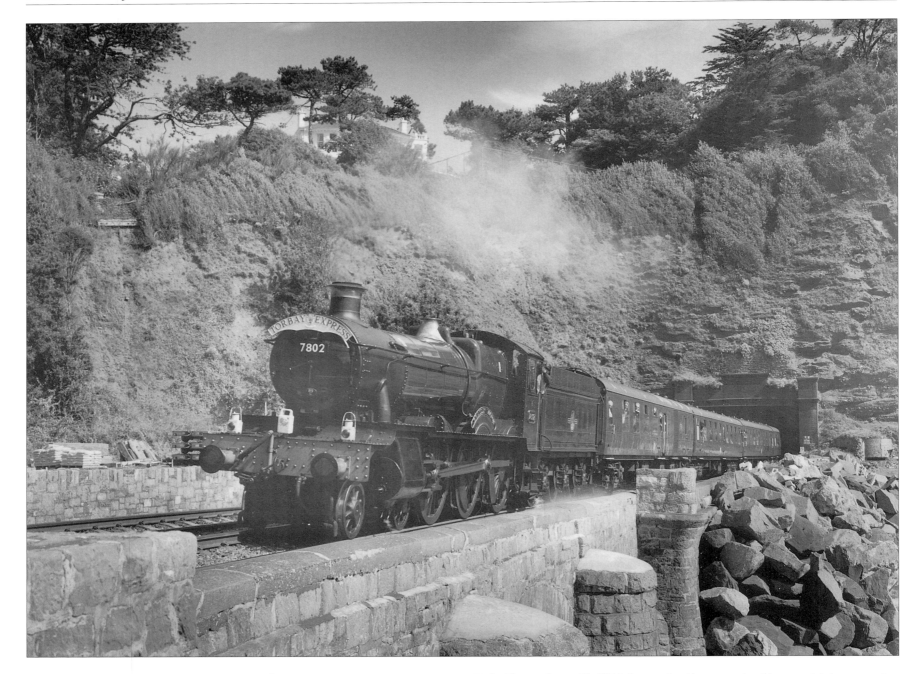

'Manor' Class

Above **Teignmouth:** Running along the famous sea wall from Dawlish on the South Devon coast, No 7802 *Bradley Manor* emerges into the sunlight at Parson's Tunnel with a Bristol Temple Meads to Paignton train. *31 August 2003*

Right **Shrewsbury:** No 7802 departs for Aberystwyth with a special day excursion train. The signal box at Severn Bridge Junction is Network Rail's largest remaining manual-lever cabin. *12 March 2005*

Above **Talerddig:** Little more than half a mile from the summit, *Bradley Manor* struggles up the 1 in 56 gradient with an Aberystwyth to Shrewsbury train. Just look at the smoke – the valley is shrouded in an absolute fog created by the exhaust from the engine! *12 March 2005*

Right **Talerddig:** Giving an ear-shattering performance, in torrential rain under a low cloud base and on a day when rail services over the line had been under threat of curtailment due to flooding, No 7802 blasts its way up the grade with an Aberystwyth to Shrewsbury train. *23 October 2004*

Southern Railway locomotives

'N15' Class

Left **Littlehampton:** Displaying the Southern Region headlamp disc code of a Portsmouth & Southsea train, No 30777 *Sir Lamiel* departs with a special from London Victoria, the first steam-hauled rail tour to visit the seaport for many years. *5 March 1995*

Below **Bolton:** Running in Southern Railway guise as No 777, *Sir Lamiel* passes on the up main with a Carnforth to Crewe train. *22 July 1991*

'S15' Class

Aynho: After stopping at Banbury for water, No 828 heads south with a Derby to Didcot special. Singled during the 1960s, double track has now been restored to the Banbury direct route via Ashendon; the down line crosses on the flyover. *11 May 1994*

Wokingham: On the former South Eastern & Chatham line, No 828 is seen with a Clapham Junction, Redhill, Guildford, Reading, Newbury, Westbury, Salisbury and Eastleigh train – an ambitious itinerary on a network devoid of watering facilities. *6 April 1997*

Above **Holmwood:** On a Sunday afternoon with the signal box switched out, locomotive No 828, having sole possession of the line, indulges itself with a run-past for photographers. The train is a Portsmouth Harbour to Clapham Junction special. *11 February 1996*

Above right **Worting Junction:** On its way up to London, No 828 crosses Battledown flyover with a Christmas shopping day-tripper for employees from Eastleigh Works, where the locomotive was built. *2 December 1995*

Right **Fenny Compton:** Diesel power gives way to steam – a stationary freight train in the up goods loop waits for No 828 to pass with a Derby to Didcot special. *11 May 1994*

'Battle of Britain' Class

Above **Canterbury West:** Reminiscent of the days when Bulleid 'Pacifics' were in their heyday on the Kent Coast expresses, No 34067 *Tangmere* heads the 'Golden Arrow' on its way to Dover, where passengers will embark for Calais. The train ferry to transport the coaching stock across the Channel is no longer available of course, but travellers on the train were still able to continue their journey, steam-hauled, to Paris, courtesy of SNCF, the French railway operating company. *14 May 2004*

Above right **Oulton Broad:** *Tangmere* is seen again this time on the East Suffolk line, with a Lowestoft to Liverpool Street train. Similar to the former Trowse structure, at Norwich, the swing bridge here is still in full working order. *18 September 2004*

Right **Worcester Shrub Hill:** One of approximately 50 Bulleid 'light Pacifics' that remained unmodified and as built in 'air-smoothed' form until withdrawal, No 34067 departs for London Victoria with the return working of a special day excursion train. *17 April 2004*

Chelsea Bridge: Soon after departure from Kensington Olympia, *Tangmere* crosses the Thames with a Canterbury West and Dover train. Probably cheaper than local apartments, the barges have been converted into house-boats. *18 July 2004*

Battersea: Designed by Giles Gilbert Scott and regarded as an architectural masterpiece, the power station building, completed in 1933, survives into the 21st century. Also built as a symbol of prestige and modernity, at Brighton in 1947, Bulleid's 'Battle of Britain' Class No 34067 passes with a London Victoria to Southampton train. *13 December 2003*

Moreton-in-Marsh: Withdrawn at Exmouth Junction in November 1963, and rescued from Barry scrapyard in January 1981, *Tangmere* arrives with a London Victoria to Worcester Shrub Hill train. *24 July 2004*

Skegness: No 34067 departs for Kings Cross with a rare steam-hauled excursion to a resort developed by the railway, to entice passengers on to trains. *10 July 2004*

'Merchant Navy' Class

Waterloo: Built at Eastleigh in 1948 and modified by British Railways in October 1959, 'Merchant Navy' Class No 35028 *Clan Line* departs for Bristol Temple Meads with a train to celebrate its golden jubilee.

Larger, of course, but as built similar to the 'Battle of Britain' 'light Pacifics' such as *Tangmere*, the appearance of both classes was completely transformed, during modification, by the removal of the 'air-smoothed' casing and the fitting of bigger chimneys. *28 March 1998*

Canterbury West: This was the first Bulleid 'Pacific' ever seen by the author, then as Southern Railway No 21C5,
at Waterloo just after the end of the Second World War. Now in its modified form, as No 35005, *Canadian Pacific* stands at Platform 2 soon after arrival
from London Victoria with a special day excursion train. *19 February 2000*

Sheriff Brow: No 35028 *Clan Line* heads north up the 'Long Drag', 10 miles from Blea Moor summit, with a Blackburn to Carlisle train. *11 May 1991*

Lillie Bridge: Displaying the Southern Region headlamp disc code of a special boat express, No 35028 passes
the London Underground permanent way depot with empty coaching stock for a Kensington Olympia to Southampton Eastern Docks private charter train.
Earls Court exhibition centre is in the background. *15 December 1996*

London Midland & Scottish Railway locomotives

5MT Class 'Mogul'

Left **Chorleywood:** Withdrawn by British Railways in December 1966 and rescued from Barry scrapyard by the Stanier Mogul Preservation Society in December 1973, No 2968 storms up the grade with a Watford to Amersham train. *24 May 1998*

Below **Chirk:** Completed in 1848, the viaduct runs next to Thomas Telford's aqueduct, opened in 1801 to carry the Shropshire Union Llangollen Canal across the valley. No 2968 passes with a Bescot to Chester train. *13 December 1997*

Left **Lickey Incline:** A moment in history – after an absence of almost 30 years, steam returns to the legendary 1 in 37¾ Worcestershire gradient as Stanier 'Mogul' No 2968 pilots Collett 'Mogul' No 7325 at Blackwell summit, with a Bristol Temple Meads to Bescot train. *22 November 1997*

5MT Class 'Black Five'

Above **Corrour:** No 45407, masquerading as former 65A Eastfield engine No 44996, heads a Fort William to Rannoch private charter train. *14 October 2004*

Left **Rugeley:** Opened in 1859, the Cannock and Rugeley line closed to passenger traffic during 1965, but services resumed to Hednesford in 1989, and to Rugeley Town in 1997, just over a year before this photograph of No 45110, on a Birmingham International to Chester train, was taken. *7 November 1998*

Above **Corrour:** Locomotive No 45407, running as No 44996, storms up the grade with a rake of six Mk I maroon coaches. Withdrawn at 67B Hurlford shed in April 1964, No 44996 was scrapped by the Shipbreaking Industries yard, Faslane, during July of that year. Former LMS 'Black Fives' worked on the West Highland line from the mid-1950s onwards. *14 October 2004*

Left **Sugar Loaf:** A severe test for both locomotives, the new partnership of No 45407 (running as No 45157) and No 76079 storm their way up towards the summit, double-heading a Newport (South Wales) to Crewe train. Withdrawn at 65B St Rollox shed during December 1962, No 45157 *The Glasgow Highlander* was scrapped by the Arnott Young yard, Troon, in January of the following year. *20 September 2003*

Above **Talerddig:** With eight bogies and steam to spare, No 45407 is seen between Llanbrynmair and the famous rock cutting with a Tywyn to Shrewsbury train. *21 March 2004*

Tebay: A partnership that was dissolved due to a series of embarrassing failures by the train engine, No 45407 pilots No 45110 on a Crewe to Carlisle special. The former Tebay engine shed remained open until the end of 1967 to provide locomotives for the Shap banking turns. *28 November 1998*

Clapham: Satirically known as the 'other' Clapham Junction until closure of the Ingleton branch to all traffic in June 1966, the origins of the line go back to the days when the Midland Railway gained access to Scotland via Ingleton and the so-called 'little North Western' route to Tebay, before the opening of the Settle and Carlisle line in 1875. Locomotive No 45407 crosses Wenning Viaduct with a Guide Bridge, Bolton, Blackburn, Hellifield, Carnforth and Crewe special. *4 March 2000*

Buxton: An engine that lasted until the very end of operational steam on British Railways, being withdrawn at 10D Lostock Hall shed on 11 August 1968, locomotive No 45110 departs for the sidings, with empty coaching stock, after arrival from Derby with a Peak Forest, Buxton and Crewe rail tour. *5 February 2000*

Castleford: Built at Crewe by the LMS in 1947 and withdrawn from service by British Railways in December 1967, No 44767 passes with a Newcastle to Manchester Victoria train. *18 March 1995*

8P 'Princess Royal' Class

Shipley: Situated on a triangle at the junction for Bradford Forster Square, the station originally only had platforms on two of its three sides, those on the main line having been added in more recent years. Until then local journeys between Leeds and Skipton necessitated a cross-platform interchange from Leeds-Bradford trains to connecting Bradford-Skipton services. No 46203 *Princess Margaret Rose* passes, on the down main, with a Derby to Carlisle special. *18 March 1994*

Artengill: Running along the backbone of England, the Settle and Carlisle line was built to give the Midland Railway its own route to Scotland, in competition with its rival the London & North Western Railway's premier line.

The viaduct is situated in real hill country, on the most isolated section of the line. No 46203 heads south with a Carlisle to Blackburn train. *20 August 1994*

8P 'Coronation' Class

Skipton: No 46229 *Duchess of Hamilton* passes the former engine shed site with a Bradford Forster Square to Appleby train. Coded 23A in its heyday during the 1950s, the shed closed completely on 3 April 1967. Formerly entrenched in the LMS complex, the railway here is now at the limit of electrification from the East Coast Main Line. *27 February 1993*

Teignmouth: During the engine's last run before withdrawal for heavy maintenance and renewal of its boiler certificate, No 6024 *King Edward I* is seen at Parson's Tunnel with a Birmingham Snow Hill to Paignton train. *26 October 2002*

Barrow Hill: This is the home of Barrow Hill Roundhouse Museum, an ex-Midland Railway steam shed opened in 1870 to provide motive power for the local mineral traffic. Known as Staveley for most of its working life, the name was changed to avoid confusion with the nearby former Great Central Railway depot. Locomotive No 6233 *Duchess of Sutherland* departs, following a water stop, with a Derby to York train. *3 April 2003*

Birkett Common: Well above the valley floor, just to the south of Kirkby Stephen, and still climbing, locomotive No 6201 *Princess Elizabeth* makes steady progress on the way up to Ais Gill, 1,169 feet above sea level, England's highest main line summit. *19 July 2003*

Sheriff Brow: No 6201 tackles the grade with a Chester to Carlisle train at the first of two short viaducts where the railway crosses a bend in the river on the northbound climb through the Ribble valley to Blea Moor summit. *12 April 2003*

Scarborough: 'Eight Freight' 2-8-0 No 48151 makes an early morning departure for York with a special excursion train.
The star on the cabside indicates that the wheels are balanced for passenger traffic duties. *7 July 2002*

Twerton: BR Standard 5MT 4-6-0 No 73096 heads west with a London Victoria to Bristol Temple Meads train. Designed by Brunel, the castellated tunnel turrets and crenellated parapet are built in Bath stone. *8 May 2003*

Kings Sutton: No 73096 passes with a London Victoria to Stratford-upon-Avon train.
The railway station here is one of only five in Northamptonshire remaining open for business. *24 July 2003*

Rannoch: Masquerading as No 61243 *Sir Harold Mitchell*, 'B1' 4-6-0 No 61264 stands in the station after arrival from Fort William piloting a Bridge of Orchy train.

Withdrawn at Ayr in May 1964, No 61243 was scrapped by the Arnott Young West of Scotland shipbreakers' yard, Troon, later that year. The other number on the cabside is the route availability code: restrictions on the working of locomotives over the routes of the former LNER were denoted by 'RA' numbers, and an engine was not permitted to work over any line of a lower reference number than itself. *6 October 2002*

Greenholme: On the unforgiving battleground of the Cumbrian fells, No 46229 works north, unassisted, over Shap with a Crewe to Carlisle train. There are plans to streamline the engine, for static display at the National Railway Museum, but it is unlikely to work on the national railway network again in the foreseeable future. *19 October 1996*

Tebay: Where she belongs, on the Glasgow-Euston main line, No 6233 *Duchess of Sutherland* is seen
just south of Dillicar, in the Lune Gorge, with a Carlisle to Carnforth train. *4 September 2004*

Scarborough: This lady *is* for turning! *Duchess of Hamilton* arrives at the terminus with a special day excursion train.

Built by the LMS at Crewe Works as a streamlined engine, No 6229 changed its name and number with No 6220 *Coronation* to visit the New York Worlds Fair in 1939, and did not return until 1943, due to the outbreak of war.

The first engine of the class, No 6220 *Coronation*, set a world record of 114mph for steam on 29 June 1937, later broken at 126mph on 3 July 1938 by LNER 'A4' No 4468 *Mallard*, a record that still stands and is unlikely to be beaten. *7 October 1995*

Left **Crowdundle:** No 6233 *Duchess of Sutherland* heads south towards Appleby with a Carlisle to Crewe special.

The engine is one of five non-streamlined 'Coronation' Class locomotives, Nos 6230-6234, built by the LMS in 1938 with curved running plates. De-streamlined engines, such as *Duchess of Hamilton*, had cut-away running plates at the front end, as did some of the later non-streamlined locomotives. After the end of the Second World War the streamlined 'Coronation' Class engines had their casings removed, and an all-black 'streak', No 6243 *City of Lancaster*, was the only example ever seen by the author. *3 July 2004*

Above **Penmaenmawr:** Not very far behind a local train that had stopped at the station, No 6233 trundles past, safety valves feathering, with a special from Crewe on the Chester and Holyhead line. *11 September 2004*

8F Class

Gobowen: Now owned by the Stanier Eight Freight Locomotive Society, No 48773 passes the Oswestry branch junction with a Shrewsbury to Blackburn train.

Probably the most famous 'Eight Freight' of them all, this locomotive was built by North British in 1940 to a War Department order; loaned to the LMS as No 8233, it was returned to the WD in 1941 and shipped to Persia. Converted to oil burning at Tehran in 1944, sent to Egypt in 1946, and returned to England in 1952, the engine was purchased by British Railways in 1957, re-numbered 48773, and converted back to coal-firing. *1 February 1992*

Ais Gill: A type of locomotive seen here in abundance during the 1940s, '50s and '60s, 'Eight Freight' No 48151 slogs past with a Carlisle, Blackburn, Preston and Carnforth train. *12 July 1996*

Disley: No 48773 heads a Crewe, Buxton and Derby rail tour. Eight miles later the locomotive slipped to a stand near Chapel-en-le-Frith and, after a call for assistance, a diesel was despatched from Buxton to pilot the train over the tortuous climb to Bibbington summit. An error in the calculation for the loading of the train was blamed. *1 April 2000*

Maltby Colliery: This was a never-to-be-repeated steam itinerary, most of it over goods lines kept open
by coal traffic from the local mines. On the South Yorkshire Joint line, No 48773 passes with a Nottingham, Pinxton, Shirebrook, Shireoaks,
Doncaster, Masborough and Derby rail tour. *16 January 1999*

London & North Eastern Railway
locomotives

'A2' Class

Left **Scarborough:** No 60532 *Blue Peter*, in back gear, propels the empty coaching stock of a private charter train from York into Platform No 1 at the terminus. It is a very long platform, but there are no run-round facilities. *26 May 1993*

Below **Seaton Carew:** With the first steam-hauled special on the national railway network in England for more than three months, after a moratorium due to the high lineside fire risk, No 60532 provides the motive power for a Middlesbrough, Sunderland, Carlisle and Preston train. *13 September 1997*

'A3' Class

Left **Bedwyn:** Just three weeks after its inaugural run following heavy maintenance and re-tubing, No 4472 *Flying Scotsman* passes with a Paddington to Salisbury train. *25 July 1999*

Above **Fenny Compton:** Seen here with a Derby to Ealing Broadway train, *Flying Scotsman* was the first steam locomotive to achieve an authenticated 100mph running speed, set in 1934 and confirmed by recording instruments in the LNER dynamometer car. The world's first 100mph with steam, recorded by *City of Truro* in 1904, was never recognised, because the Great Western Railway could not prove it. *21 October 1992*

Bath Spa: No 4472 departs with a Bristol to London train. The abbey church is obscured by smoke from the engine, but the spire of St John the Evangelist stands proud above the skyline. *31 March 2001*

Worcester Shrub Hill: *Flying Scotsman* leaves with the return working of a special day excursion train. A pioneer during its early years of preservation, there was a time in the late 1960s when No 4472 was the only steam locomotive permitted to work on the national railway network. *23 June 2001*

Battersea: Withdrawn at Kings Cross in January 1963, and now boasting more than 40 years of running as a preserved main line locomotive, *Flying Scotsman*, the pride of the old LNER, passes with a London Victoria to Salisbury train. *8 November 2003*

Salisbury: English heritage at its best – the magnificent cathedral, built from Chilmark stone, and No 4472 *Flying Scotsman* departing with a London Victoria to Westbury train. Some of the stone for the cathedral was taken from the Roman fortress at Old Sarum, where only foundations remain. *4 April 2001*

'A4' Class

Kings Cross: 'Sir Nigel Gresley designed his A4, The speed of a greyhound, the strength of a boar.' Named after the designer himself, locomotive No 60007 departs for Doncaster with a special to celebrate the 40th anniversary of its 112mph post-war steam record. *23 May 1999*

Tebay: Believed to be the first steam-hauled train over the Lancaster and Carlisle line for 27 years, *Sir Nigel Gresley* heads north with a Crewe to Carlisle special.

All appears to be well, but there had been problems at Preston earlier in the day when the steam siren whistle valve jammed open, and a poor performance by the engine was attributed to the wrong kind of coal, Daw Mill nuggets, instead of cobbles. *30 September 1995*

Durham: 'Out of York city and on to the north, Past Durham, Newcastle, over Tweed, to the Forth.' High above the rows of terraced houses huddled around the viaduct, No 60009 *Union of South Africa* coasts down the grade with a luncheon special dining car train from York on the East Coast Main Line. *5 June 2004*

Waterloo: No 60009 leaves the terminus with a special for Salisbury. There have been other visits to Waterloo by the 'A4' Class, of course, most notably that of *Mallard* during the 1948 engine exchange trials. *22 January 1995*

High Scales: Running almost parallel to the M6 motorway, observed by motorists slowing down to get a better view,
No 60007 approaches Scout Green with a Crewe to Carlisle train. *18 April 1998*

Tebay: Taking up the gauntlet between the electrics and other high-speed trains, No 60009 heads south through the Lune Gorge with a Carlisle to Preston special. *2 August 2003*

Above **Crowdundle:** On New Year's Day, at the old county boundary between Westmorland and Cumberland in the new county of Cumbria, *Sir Nigel Gresley*, carrying its LNER number 4498, heads south with a Carlisle to Blackburn train. *1 January 1993*

Right **Ais Gill:** Running in LNER garter blue livery with a Carlisle to Blackburn train, No 4498 (later BR No 60007) crosses the short viaduct spanning the narrow mountain stream. *8 May 1993*

Settle Junction: A month after the spring equinox, the trees in the Dales are still bare as No 60009 drifts down the grade towards the junction with a Carlisle to Crewe train. *20 April 2002*

Lakenheath: Semaphore track circuit block signalling sees *Union of South Africa* on its way from Kings Cross to Norwich Thorpe with a special day excursion train. Expresses from Liverpool Street hauled by British Railways Standard 'Pacifics' could be seen here during the 1950s and '60s. *11 October 2003*

'B1' Class

Corrour: Running as No 61244 *Strang Steel*, No 61264 pounds its way up towards the summit, across the barren landscape of the moors, with a private charter train. *4 October 2003*

Loch Eilt: On the iron road to the isles, No 61264 heads a Fort William to Mallaig summer timetable day excursion train.
ScotRail passengers wishing to travel in one direction only could upgrade their tickets by payment of a special supplement. *3 October 2003*

Auch: No 61264 (masquerading as No 61244) crosses Horseshoe viaduct with a Fort William to Crianlarich private charter train. Formerly a 64A St Margaret's engine, No 61244 was named after the late Samuel Strang Steel, an LNER Director. *4 October 2003*

Upper Tyndrum: Beneath the lofty dignity of Beinn Dorain, 3,524 feet above sea level, on the tortuous climb through the Grampians, No 61264 (as 61244) is seen at County March summit with the Fort William to Crianlarich private charter train. *4 October 2003*

Rannoch Moor: No 61264 (still as 61244) heads south towards the Cruach snowshed with a rake of five Mk I coaches. Withdrawn by British Railways on 29 October 1965, No 61244 *Strang Steel* was scrapped in December of that year at the Shipbreaking Industries yard, Faslane. *5 October 2003*

Allington Junction: No 61264 arrives from Grantham via Barkston East, an early morning light engine movement in connection with a Grantham and Immingham rail tour. *25 October 2003*

Weaverthorpe: No 61264 passes with a Doncaster to Scarborough special day excursion train. Later in the day the engine blew a
small boiler tube, delaying the arrival back at Doncaster, diesel-hauled, until 2355 instead of 1915; those passengers that enjoyed the full itinerary,
from Kings Cross, returned to the capital at 0345 on Sunday morning ! *13 March 2004*

Ingatestone: No 61264 passes with a Liverpool Street to Norwich Thorpe excursion. On arrival at its destination
the steam locomotive had an overheated driving wheel bearing, and the train returned to London diesel-hauled. *10 November 2001*

'K1' Class

Corrour: Apparently the sanders were not working, and the driver only just managed to prevent the train coming to a stand when the locomotive slipped on the climb through the Monessie gorge earlier in the day. There are no leaves on the line up here, however, and No 62005 (running as No 62012) makes a sure-footed ascent with a Spean Bridge to Rannoch private charter train. *10 October 2004*

Corrour: In driving rain, under leaden skies, running as erstwhile 65J Fort William engine No 62052,
No 62005 slogs up the grade from Loch Treig with a Fort William to Crianlarich train. *8 October 2003*

Whitby: Built across the Esk valley for the Scarborough & Whitby Railway in 1885, and closed to all traffic on 8 March 1965,
the barriers across Larpool Viaduct have been removed since the photograph was taken, and the route is now open again for cyclists and walkers.
Locomotive No 62005 departs with a Middlesbrough train – there was a permanent way restriction on the line as far as Grosmont,
so it was never going to be a full-regulator performance. *10 October 1999*

Loch Eilt: No 62005, running as No 62012, passes with a Mallaig to Fort William train. Withdrawn at Sunderland in May 1967, the original No 62012 was scrapped by Draper's of Hull on 28 August 1967. Usually the number change is indiscernible, but on this occasion the alteration can be clearly seen on the cab-side. *9 October 2004*

Loch Awe: No 62005, this time in the guise of No 62052, crosses the viaduct at the eastern end of the water with an Oban to Crianlarich train.
Withdrawn by British Railways on 29 December 1962, No 62052 was stored at Bo'ness until April 1964, when it was sent to Cowlairs for cutting up. *8 October 2003*

Gilberdyke: At this important junction in the East Riding of Yorkshire, No 62005 passes the old Staddlethorpe railway cottages with a York to Hull train on the down main from Selby; the Goole line joins from the left. *23 February 2002*

'V2' Class

Hellifield: After running round its support coach in the down goods loop, No 4771 (British Railways No 60800) departs in back gear for Blackburn, where it will take over a Settle and Carlisle train brought in from the south by a diesel. The origin and destination of the trains featured in this volume are given for the steam-hauled sections only; very few rail tours are steam-hauled throughout, and most have either diesel or electric traction included in the itinerary. *25 July 1992*

Clay Cross South Junction: Carrying its BR number, No 60800 heads north from Derby with a Banbury to York train. The junction is 142 miles from St Pancras via the Erewash Valley line, which joins here on the left, the route north via Derby being just over 5 miles longer. *16 June 2001*

Left **Scarborough:** No 60800 departs for York with 'The Scarborough Spa Express' day-tripper. Probably bigger than a similar survivor at nearby Bridlington, the signal box is certainly one of the largest remaining former North Eastern Railway cabins. *28 May 2001*

Above **Scarborough:** A 'pivotal' moment for No 60800 on the turntable that was provided by the local authority after British Railways agreed to run a series of steam specials to the resort. *28 May 2001*

British Railways Standard locomotives

4MT Class

Left **Loch Eilt:** Running tender-first, Standard 4-6-0 No 75014 passes with a Mallaig to Fort William train. There is now a turntable at Fort William, but plans for another at Mallaig are in disarray. *26 August 1997*

Below **Loch Dubh:** Locomotive No 75014 heads towards Arisaig, the most westerly point on the national railway network, with a Fort William to Mallaig train. The re-aligned A830 trunk road now overlooks this position from the other side of the water. *26 August 1996*

Chorleywood: No 75014 storms up the grade with a Watford to Amersham train. British Railways Standard locomotives could be seen here almost every day during the late 1950s and early '60s hauling semi-fasts to Nottingham and expresses to Sheffield over the old Great Central route from Marylebone. The end came on 4 September 1966, when the line between Calvert and Rugby Central closed to all traffic. *26 May 1996*

Chorleywood: 'Steam on the Met', the annual festival organised by London Underground, ceased at the start of the new millennium and scenes like this are now denied to us. Locomotive No 75014 passes with an Amersham to Watford train. *19 May 1996*

4MT Class 'Mogul'

Helwith Bridge: No 76079 pilots 'Black Five' No 45407 on a Manchester Victoria to Carlisle train over the northbound climb to Blea Moor summit. Both of the engines are owned by Ian Riley, the Bury, Lancashire, steam entrepreneur. *26 March 2005*

Crowdundle: Running as former 71A Eastleigh 'Mogul' No 76029, No 76079 pilots 'Battle of Britain' Class No 34067 *Tangmere* as they double-head a Carlisle to Preston train.

Built in 1953 at Doncaster, the original No 76029 had a very short working life; withdrawn from Eastleigh on 4 October 1964, it was stored there until February 1965, and scrapped at Cohen's Morriston yard, Swansea, in March of that year.

The engines pictured here have only worked together in preservation, but after the first Somerset & Dorset Joint line test run of a Standard 4MT 'Mogul' on 5 March 1955, this class of locomotive occasionally piloted Bulleid 'light Pacifics' over that route, hence the 'Pines Express' headboard. Inappropriate headlamp disc codes were sometimes a feature of S&DJR running, such as the one displayed here, for a Southampton Docks and Salisbury train. *21 February 2004*

4MT Class Tank

Mitre Bridge: On the West London line, 2-6-4T No 80079 passes with a Christmas excursion from Kensington Olympia.
Note the Eurostar train at the North Pole servicing and inspection shed in the background. *18 December 1994*

Sleaford: Sister loco No 80080 arrives with a Skegness train on the Boston, Sleaford and Midland Counties line. An important junction in rural Lincolnshire, this station was spared many of the drastic reductions in rail services suffered by neighbouring communities as a result of the Beeching Report. *2 April 1994*

5MT Class

Above **Crofton:** Standard 4-6-0 No 73096 works up the grade towards Savernake with a London Victoria to Westbury train. Originally a rival of the Kennet & Avon Canal, the Great Western Railway later owned it, when all competition ceased and the waterway was allowed to fall into disrepair. *6 September 2003*

Right **Battersea:** Earlier in the day, soon after departure from London Victoria, No 73096 threads its way through the suburbs with the Westbury train. A listed Grade II building, the power station stopped generating electricity in 1983, and planning permission has been granted for change of use to leisure-based activities. *6 September 2003*

Bursledon: Displaying the Southern Region headlamp disc code of a Southampton and Salisbury train,
No 73096 passes with a special from Guildford on the Netley line. *15 March 1998*

Foxton: On the Shepreth branch, No 73096 heads a Finsbury Park to Lincoln train. The former signal cabin has been retained as a gate box at this busy A10 trunk road level crossing. *4 December 2004*

7P Class

Norton Junction: No 70000 *Britannia* is photographed on a Taunton to Worcester Shrub Hill train.
Plans for a divergence here, instead of a junction, have been abandoned. *25 July 1993*

Ely: Displaying the standard express passenger headlamp disc code, No 70000 is on its way from Cambridge
to Kings Lynn with 'The Fenman' special day excursion train. *19 October 1991*

8P Class

Amberley: On the third rail Southern Region electrified network, No 71000 *Duke of Gloucester* pounds its way up the grade towards North Stoke Tunnel with a London Victoria to Chichester train. *18 December 2004*

Settle: Never highly regarded by London Midland Region enginemen, who much preferred the 'Coronation' Class 'Pacifics',
Duke of Gloucester has become one of Britain's most successful preserved locomotives, having comfortably defeated *Duchess of Hamilton* to win the Shap time trials.
Locomotive No 71000 is seen here with a Preston to Carlisle train. *1 May 2005*

Tebay: Soon after returning to the main line following a prolonged absence, due to unforeseen problems encountered during heavy maintenance for renewal of its boiler certificate, No 71000 heads north through the Lune Gorge with a Preston to Carlisle train. *10 September 2004*

Directory of featured locomotives

Class	Locomotive		Built	Wheel arrangement	Pages
Great Western Railway locomotives					
'City'	3440	*City of Truro*	1903 Swindon	4-4-0	1, 6-9
'Hall'	4936	*Kinlet Hall*	1929 Swindon	4-6-0	13, 14
	4965	*Rood Ashton Hall*	1929 Swindon	4-6-0	10-13, 15
'Castle'	5029	*Nunney Castle*	1934 Swindon	4-6-0	17-23
	5051	*Drysllwyn Castle/Earl Bathurst*	1936 Swindon	4-6-0	16, 18 , 22
'King'	6024	*King Edward I*	1930 Swindon	4-6-0	23-25, colour i
'4300'	7325		1932 Swindon	2-6-0	26-29, 52
'Manor'	7802	*Bradley Manor*	1938 Swindon	4-6-0	30-33
'9400'	9466		1953 Robert Stephenson & Hawthorns Ltd	0-6-0PT	27
Southern Railway locomotives					
'N15'	30777	*Sir Lamiel*	1925 North British	4-6-0	34, 35
'S15'	828		1927 Eastleigh	4-6-0	36-39
'Battle of Britain'	34067	*Tangmere*	1947 Brighton	4-6-2	40-45, 115
'Merchant Navy'	35005	*Canadian Pacific*	1941 Eastleigh	4-6-2	47
	35028	*Clan Line*	1948 Eastleigh	4-6-2	46, 48, 49
London Midland & Scottish Railway locomotives					
5MT 'Mogul'	2968		1934 Crewe	2-6-0	50-52
5MT 'Black Five'	44767		1947 Crewe	4-6-0	61
	45110		1935 Vulcan Foundry	4-6-0	54, 58, 60
	45407		1937 Armstrong Whitworth	4-6-0	53, 55-59, 114
8P 'Princess Royal'	6201	*Princess Elizabeth*	1933 Crewe	4-6-2	colour iii, colour iv
	46203	*Princess Margaret Rose*	1935 Crewe	4-6-2	62, 63
8P 'Coronation'	46229	*Duchess of Hamilton*	1938 Crewe	4-6-2	64, 65, 67
	6233	*Duchess of Sutherland*	1938 Crewe	4-6-2	66, 68, 69, colour ii
8F	48151		1942 Crewe	2-8-0	71, colour v
	48773		1940 North British	2-8-0	70, 72, 73
London & North Eastern Railway locomotives					
'A2'	60532	*Blue Peter*	1948 Doncaster	4-6-2	74, 75
'A3'	4472	*Flying Scotsman*	1923 Doncaster	4-6-2	76-81
'A4'	60007	*Sir Nigel Gresley*	1937 Doncaster	4-6-2	82, 83, 86, 88, 89
	60009	*Union of South Africa*	1937 Doncaster	4-6-2	2, 84, 85, 87, 90, 91
'B1'	61264		1947 North British	4-6-0	92-99, colour viii
'K1'	62005		1949 North British	2-6-0	100-105
'V2'	60800	*Green Arrow*	1936 Doncaster	2-6-2	106-109
British Railways Standard locomotives					
4MT	75014		1951 Swindon	4-6-0	110-113
4MT 'Mogul'	76079		1957 Horwich	2-6-0	56, 114, 115
4MT Tank	80079		1954 Brighton	2-6-4T	116
	80080		1954 Brighton	2-6-4T	117
5MT	73096		1955 Derby	4-6-0	118-121, colour vi, colour vii
7P	70000	*Britannia*	1951 Crewe	4-6-2	122, 123
8P	71000	*Duke of Gloucester*	1954 Crewe	4-6-2	124-126

Index of locations

Acknowledgements

For their help in compiling this book, the author would like to thank Peter Townsend, Mick Sanders and Will Adams of Silver Link Publishing Ltd, Chris Banks for access to his locomotive archive records, Jeff Cogan for providing the lineside timings, and the locomotive owners, tour operators and railwaymen of all grades whose professionalism made it possible.